THE ARCS
OF INFINITY

POCKET EDITION

Published from
Mardukite Borsippa HQ, San Luis Valley, Colorado
Mardukite Academy & Systemology Society
for spiritual or educational purposes only

THE ARCS OF INFINITY

Systemology
Professional Course
Booklet #15

Developed by Joshua Free
for the Systemology Society

ISBN : 978-1-961509-40-5

Pocket Paperback Edition — *December 2023*

mardukite.com

Chart Your Flight For Ascension...
Then Let Your Spirit Fly!

Unlock your ultimate spiritual potential by removing barriers to your true native state.

Learn how to easily attain Self-actualization and help to actualize others along the way.

A greater appreciation and understanding of *Spiritual Life* and *Existence* awaits you. Expand your reach to achieve your dreams.

Each 'Professional Course' lesson-booklet offers simple exercises and techniques that directly apply the philosophy of Systemology, assisting to increase your true knowingness, improve your capabilities in this life, and even decide what you will do in your next.

At the Mardukite Academy of Systemology, the 'Professional Course' lessons in this series are presented to Seeker's that have already completed the 'Basic Course', previously released as six lesson-booklets, or the six-in-one single volume edition "Fundamentals of Systemology."

This all new presentation of the Systemology 'Pathway-to-Ascension' takes Seekers and continuing students from "Zero" to "Infinity" at lightning-fast speeds!

Discover Who You Really Are...
Because You Were Never Human

TABLET OF CONTENTS

COURSE INTRODUCTION

LESSON FIFTEEN:
THE ARCS OF INFINITY

APPENDIX

PROFESSIONAL
COURSE
INTRODUCTION

WELCOME, SEEKER!
LET'S CHART YOUR JOURNEY
ON THE PATHWAY

Systemology is a "holistic" approach to understanding the human experience. It is not actually a singular "subject" in itself, but rather, a new way in which to view the many subjects of *Life* and all *Existence.*

This is a professional course in *Systemology*—specifically, how to *apply* the spiritual philosophy of *Mardukite Systemology* as a personal "*Pathway*" to *Ascension.* Our *Systemology* is a new approach to "*Self-Actualization.*" It is completely relevant for the modern age and the future, and quite different from any previous similar attempts, or other traditions, you might find. What's more: it is applicable to anyone with any background.

This *"Professional Course"* series of lessons (booklets) immediately follows the material given in the *"Basic Course"* series—available as six separate pocket-sized booklets, or in a single hardcover volume titled: *"Fundamentals of Systemology: A New Thought For The 21st Century."*

This is a *new* presentation of *Systemology*, emphasizing the application of our philosophy for those *Seekers* that are *"Flying-Solo"*—or else working through their studies and exercises as solitary practitioners. This is a new innovation for *Systemology*. Aside from the book *"Crystal Clear,"* all of our former advanced courses have placed a focus on *"Traditional Piloting"*—where experienced practitioners assist *Seekers* in *"processing."*

To receive the greatest benefit from this study: it is expected that a *Seeker* will already be familiar with the fundamental concepts and terminology (previously relayed in the *Basic Course*) before using lessons from the *Professional Course*. This will allow us to cover the extensive territory of the *Pathway* much more quickly. However, for reference, a basic "*glossary*" of vocabulary used in this lesson is provided in the "*appendix*."

A NEW VIEW OF THE HUMAN SPIRIT

Systemology is not a religion and does not require any type of *faith*. It is, however, built upon a "spiritual" premise—and as such is an "applied spiritual philosophy." It is based on ancient teachings that we are *Spiritual Beings* essentially "wearing" bodies like clothes—or using them as "vehicles." Yet our true native nature is not *physical*, but beyond this existence; and we can certainly operate a "body" from *outside* of it.

We are **all** *Spiritual Beings*—each of us a *unit* of *Spiritual Awareness*—that have experienced a very long *Spiritual Timeline* of existence. Although we might be particularly attached to the familiar "physical shells" associated with *this* lifetime, our true *"Spiritual Lifetime"* is seemingly *eternal*. We have been many things before *Human*, and we go onward as a *Spiritual Being* after our *"genetic vehicle"* of *this* incarnation perishes.

While a "spiritual" view of the *Human Condition* may not seem unique to our philosophy, just how often is the concept treated *systematically*? For that matter: just how many people, supposedly raised to this or that religion, or professing to believe one thing or another, actually live their lives as though they are *Spirits?*

As *Spiritual Beings* of immortal existence and infinite potential, we are not simply the *"creations"* of an even greater *Being-*

ness; we are, in fact, an integral part of that *"creative force"* which permeates all existence.

Our basic nature is to be a *"creative being"* —our highest goals are *"to create."* And as such a being—which we refer to as an *Alpha-Spirit* in *Systemology*—we have run into some difficulties along the course of our *Spiritual Timeline* and found ourselves trapped within material *Universes* of our own collaborative *creation*.

Since we did not start out our existence in a trapped condition, it is correct to say that we have *"fallen"* from our native *"godlike"* states. It did not happen all at one, but progressively and systematically. We know our "troubles" have resulted from accumulated "barriers" and "blockages" —or *fragmentation*—during our vast experiences as *Spiritual Beings*. They are not because we lack something; but because of what's been added.

In *Systemology*, we systematically examine those routes by which we must have descended to reach our present condition, then reverse the direction of travel and chart a personal *"Pathway to Ascension."* Of course, the exact "details" of the *Spiritual Timeline* will be different for each individual *Seeker*. However, we have been able to systematically chart our *Pathway* based on common patterns of *Human fragmentation*.

In the most basic terms: the *fragmentation* that defines our "downward spiral" consists of decisions or considerations where we deny our true nature. This includes those decisions to *"withdraw"* rather than *"reach"*; where we choose to *not-know* rather than *know*; to *not-communicate* rather than *communicate*; and ultimately, to take *no-responsibility* for being a *creative-cause*, and therefore succumb to being an *effect*.

But there is *hope!* And much more importantly: there is an effectively workable *way out* of the mazes and traps of our existence. If you are reading this now, you have already begun to gather your tools and build up the *"horsepower"* necessary to break the gravity holding your *Spiritual Beingness* to the *Human Condition.*

STUDYING THE PROFESSIONAL COURSE

Most *Seekers* study and practice *Systemology* at-a-distance and independent of the "Mardukite Academy" or any "Master-level" mentors trained therein. This means that the *books* (and to a lesser degree, the *internet*) are the only means of direct contact a *Seeker* maintains with the "Systemology Society" during their studies. A continuing *Seeker* from the *"Basic Course"* will be familiar with the style of study found in *this* course.

Misunderstood words are the most common reason an individual abandons studying a subject. When a misunderstanding occurs, *Awareness* declines. These misunderstandings start to "stack up" after the first occurrence, and as a result, the level of interest and attention will also decline. This is how a "confusion" develops; and the individual will get "bored" with the subject, feel tired, and unable to concentrate.

One solution is to return to the part of the material that was still interesting and enjoyable to read. When scanning around that area of text, there is likely to be a new word (or new specific use of a familiar word) that is unclear, but was passed by unnoticed. All *Systemology* books include their own *glossary*. Using this *glossary* and a high-quality dictionary will help resolve this misunderstanding once it is located.

An effective education of any subject is taught on a *gradient*. This is what is intended by presenting the study of something as *"grades."* Rather than treating a subject as one total mass, true learning is achieved by increasing one's understanding with a *gradual* increase upward. The *ascent* to a mountaintop is not successfully achieved in one leap, but by targeting and reaching specific checkpoints along the way.

This *Professional Course* consists of a series of lessons (booklets) that gradually increase a *Seeker's* ability to understand and apply the practices and techniques of *Systemology* as a complete *"Pathway to Ascension."* It is an appropriate study for continuing *Seekers* (from the *Basic Course*), but also "advanced" *Systemologists*.

Each lesson (booklet) of the *Professional Course* applies *Systemology* to a particular subject (or focus). It is best if the entire course can be studied and applied in sequential order. These lessons also employ a style of practice or technique called *"Systematic Processing."* An introduction to applying this methodology is provided in the final lesson (booklet) of the *Basic Course*—or in the *"Fundamentals of Systemology"* volume.

To study the *Professional Course* just like a student at the Academy: a *Seeker* reads through all instructional material and applies each exercise (or *"process"*) presented in the text to the extent they comfortably can, before continuing on to the next lesson (booklet).

When first starting on the *Pathway* as a *Solo* practitioner, without the aid of an experienced *Pilot*, a *Seeker* shouldn't "push too hard" or allow themselves to get too "stuck" on any one area (lesson) or *process*. It is not expected that any one area will be completely handled when first introduced. For optimum results, it is expected that a serious *Seeker* will make more than one "pass" through the entire *Professional Course*.

The *Professional Course* is not altogether different from other forms of practical or technical education: where the instruction and exercises are delivered to a completion, and then a student further increases their abilities, strength and skill-level by applying additional practice throughout their life. Therefore, a student should not concern themselves with perfectly mastering each step (or lesson) before progressing forward.

Additional passes through the material are likely to result in different *"realizations"* (an increased *level of understanding*) than a previous time. New "layers" of *Knowingness* may now be accessible during a *process* that may not have been before. It is important to avoid invalidating

21

the progress you've made just because one area is not completely handled right away, or if a certain *process* seems too difficult on the first pass.

CHARTING A COURSE ON THE PATHWAY

Although we can communicate a systematic structure to *fragmentation,* the personal journey experienced along the *Pathway* will be different for each *Seeker.* For example, certain areas will seem more "*turbulent*" or difficult for one *Seeker* than another. We tend to say that these areas have more "*charge*" on them—or that they are more "*heavily charged.*" It is best to handle such areas when you are already feeling "good" and not in a situation (or condition) where that specific area is consistently being "*triggered*" or "*restimulated.*"

As an applied philosophy, *Systemology* "theory" can be easily utilized in the "laboratory" of the "world-at-large" in everyday life. This is implied within the basic instruction of each lesson. Unlike other "sciences" that conduct experiments by making a change to some "objective variable" *out there* and waiting to see an effect, our focus is the individual (or *Observer*) themselves, and how *they* affect the "*Reality*" perceived.

In addition to applying *Systemology* "New Thought" to everyday life, our philosophy is applied by using specific exercises and systematic techniques. These "*processes*" provide the most stable personal gain (and *realizations*) for each area; but only when actually applied with a *Seeker's* full "*presence*" and *Awareness*.

This *Professional Course* is designed so that it may be easily read and studied with little concern for what "dangers"

23

these teachings—or *processing*—might unleash. However, there are still some guidelines that pertain to the "best-uses" of these course lessons, particularly if a *Seeker* intends for stable development.

Skipping over too much material/*processing* in early lessons may make attempts to understand (or apply) later lessons more difficult. However, once the complete *Professional Course* is worked through at least once in its entirety, specific areas can then be later returned to and treated with a greater sense of *Awareness* and "*presence*" than before. Of course, in "*Traditional Piloting*," the rate of processing is monitored by an experienced practitioner; but in "*Solo-Processing*," a *Seeker* must regulate their own progress on the *Pathway*.

Applying a systematic technique is called "*running a process*." The *processes* are designed with very simple instructions or "command-lines." To run a processing command-line, a Seeker may be assisted by the communication of that line from a "Co-Pilot" (as in "Traditional Piloting"). But even then, a Seeker must still personally "input" the command as Self. For this reason —and quite thankfully— Solo-Processing is possible.

TAKING FLIGHT ON THE PATHWAY

Processing Techniques are intended to treat the Spiritual Being or Alpha-Spirit; the individual themselves. It is applied by the Alpha-Spirit—then Self-directed to the "Mind-System" or even a "body" (genetic-vehicle), both of which are "constructs" that the Alpha-Spirit (Self, or the "I-AM" Awareness unit) operates, but neither of which is actually Self. Fragmentation causes Humans to falsely identify Self as the "Mind" or even a "Body."

The *Professional Course* lessons (booklets) are designed for the *Beginning Seeker* in mind—one that may have an understanding of theory, but with little experience in practice. That being said: each of these lessons may be used toward total *Beta-Defragmentation* within a specific area. There are also more *processes* given for each subject than may be necessary to achieve an *ultimate end-point realization* on that entire area.

Some *processes* can be treated quite lightly at first; others may require a bit of working at in order to get *"running"* well. It is important to set aside a period of time when you can be dedicated to your studies and *processing*. This period of time is referred to as a *"processing session."* The reason for this, is that when a *process* does start *running* well, it is important to be able to complete it to a satisfactory *"end-point."*

The purpose of *systematic processing* is to be able to *really* "look" at things and even determine the *considerations* we have made—or attitudes we have decided—about *Reality* as a result of those experiences. It doesn't do us much good to simply "glance"—or to *restimulate* something uncomfortable and then quickly *withdraw* from it once again, leaving more of our *attention* yet again behind and held fixedly on it.

Generally speaking, a *Seeker* continues to *run* a *process* so long as something is "happening"—which is to say, the *process* is still producing a change. Usually this is evident by the type of "answers" that a *command-line* helps a *Seeker* originate from the database of their own *Mind-System*. The *command-lines* do not "do" anything on their own. They assist a *Seeker* to direct their own attention toward increasing *Awareness*.

Of course, a *Seeker* may also cease to generate new "data" from a *process* without reaching an *"ultimate" realization* as an *"end-point."* It is possible that additional "layers" (or even other "areas") require handling before anything "deeper" is accessible. If this is the case, end the *process*. But, if a *Seeker* is *withdrawing* from something uncomfortable that was incited or stirred up, then a *process* is *run* until they feel "good" about it.

In case the thought of encountering *"turbulence"* is a concern: the techniques given as *"Opening Procedures"* of a *Formal Session* (in the *Basic Course*), and those found in the earliest lessons of the *Professional Course*, are quite useful when applied as "safety nets" for maintaining *Awareness* and *presence*, even when *Flying-Solo*.

One of the benefits to *Flying-Solo* is that *processing* is entirely *Self-determined*. This already provides a certain built-in "safety" for a practitioner. Anything you *restimulate* by *Self-determinism* is *your thing*. It is not incited by external *other-determined* influences (or other "source-points" in existence) that make you an *effect*. It can be more easily handled in *processing*—or you can simply let things "cool down" and come back to it again.

While it may seem "mysterious" to beginners, a *Seeker* gets a sense for knowing how long to *run* a *process* only with practice. Once you have spent some time actually applying the *Professional Course*, there are many aspects that become "second nature" because they are, in fact, a part of our true original nature. All we have done is *"reverse engineer"* the routes of *creation* and *consideration* that are already *our own*.

LESSON FIFTEEN:
THE ARCS OF
INFINITY

SPHERES OF EXISTENCE

Here in the second-to-last lesson (booklet) of the *Professional Course*, we move quickly through some more *advanced* concepts regarding the *Human Condition,* the *Game of Life*, and *Universes*. The lesson continues with areas treated previously. They are "*advanced*"; not because they are necessarily "*complex*" or difficult to understand, but because a *Seeker* is likely to have a greater appreciation for, or understanding of, them now—and how they might apply to one's own future progress on the *Pathway*.

Let's begin with the fact that we have no actual concern or question of the ongoing "existence" of an *Alpha-Spirit*. The *Spirit,* is as they say, "*Eternal*" or "*Immortal*." It is the "*conditions*" that one considers *as existence* that seem to decline and dwindle with each more *fragmented Universe* and each more *fragmented Lifetime.*

The *implanted-goal* of *this* present *Game-Universe* is *"To Survive"* —but that doesn't mean there is nothing else for an individual to pursue; it means that our *participation* in, and *experience* of, this level of *game* requires us to simultaneously apply *efforts* toward actively maintaining the *survival* of an *"organic game-piece."* It is from *this* perspective (in *Beta-Existence*) that we consider the *"Spheres of Existence"* (as first introduced in the *Basic Course* lessons regarding the *"Fundamentals of Systemology"*).

From our perspective as a *Human Body* (or as a *lifeform* on *Earth*), the *Spheres of Existence* represent the various existing *fields* or *game-boards* that "spread out" in *Beta-Existence* from the *"Body."* We typically label the *First Sphere,* "SELF" (again, for perspective)—but what it really means for *this game* of *Beta-Existence* is:

survival through a *Body* as an individual *"player."* It is only *as a "Body"* that we have any *"need to survive."*

The other *Spheres* are all *"aids"* or *"to one's own individual *survival"*; yet those that we consider as living their lives *"seemingly oblivious"* to others, would not have much *Awareness* extending beyond the *First Sphere*. It is easy to see, however, just how important these other *Spheres* are, as *"dynamic systems"* aiding *survival* of a *Body* (or individual).

1: PHYSICAL BODY; to meet the organic needs of a living organism.
2: HOME; to meet the domestic needs; housing, intimate relationships, sexuality, and procreation (physical survival continuing by future generations).
3: GROUPS; to meet social needs and participation with others (toward goals); includes jobs, clubs, and organizations.
4: SPECIES; to *exist/survive* as the *Human* species collectively.

5: LIFE ON EARTH; *survival* as a *lifeform* on *Earth*; *survival of* the *Earth*; includes *all living beings* on the *planet,* such as trees, animals and ecosystems.

6: PHYSICAL UNIVERSE; *survival* as a *lifeform* in *Beta-Existence*; *survival of* the *Physical Universe*; includes *all* the *space-time, energy-matter,* and *organic-life* of *this Physical Universe.*

7: METAPHYSICAL; the higher-level (*Alpha*) non-physical (often less obvious) influences of *Beta-Existence*; often limited to considerations of *"thought,"* but actually includes *all entities* and *spiritual fragments.*

8: INFINITY; is always *Infinity*, the ultimate *Alpha source*—but from the perspective of *Beta-Existence*, it tends to represent *"God"* or *"Divinity"* as the *source-point* of *Beta-Existence*; hence *Humans* tend to only approach this from the perspective of *"religion"* and *"worship."*

Before looking at this further, let's do some *light processing.* For this, you will

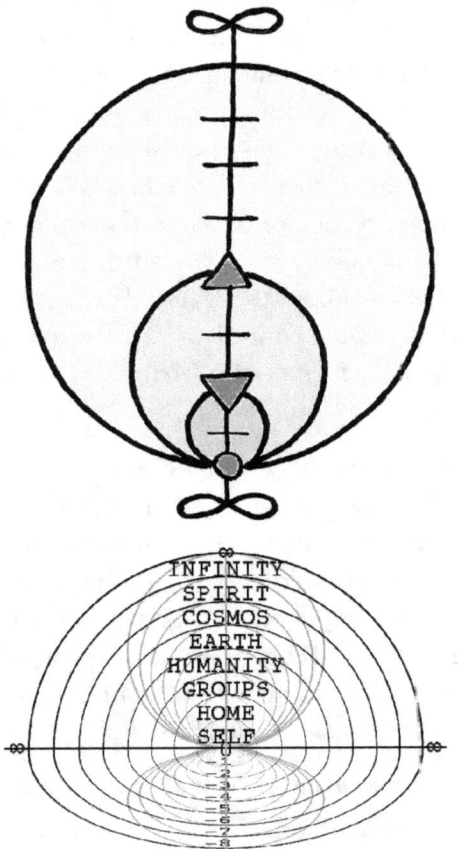

∞
INFINITY
SPIRIT
COSMOS
EARTH
HUMANITY
GROUPS
HOME
SELF
∞ ⎯⎯⎯⎯⎯⎯⎯⎯ 0 ⎯⎯⎯⎯⎯⎯⎯⎯ ∞
-1
-2
-3
-4
-5
-6
-7
-8

37

simply list your considerations in your note-book (or *Flight-Log*). It should be understood by this point of the whole course that we *process* our *considerations systematically* in order to *"free"* them from any particular *fixation* or *limitation*. We aren't *running* an idea or concept to the point of *apathy* (*"unfeelingness"*); we bring *Self-Determination* about those *considerations* back under greater control of *Self* by treating them *knowingly* (with *Actualized Awareness*).

The following *processing command-lines* ("PCL") use the word *"could"* so that we are not restricting the *considerations* to what has/hasn't or is/isn't happening, *&tc.* We simply want a *Seeker* to explore these areas. [For present purposes: by *"survival,"* we mean the *continuance* of *game-experience* in *Beta-Existence*.]

A. *"How could a 'body' aid your survival?"*

B. *"How could you aid the survival of a 'body'?"*

38

A. *"How could 'family' or 'partners' aid your survival?"*

B. *"How could you aid the survival of your 'family' or 'partners'?"*

A. *"How could a 'group' you are a part of aid your survival?"*

B. *"How could you aid the survival of a 'group' you are a part of?"*

A. *"How could 'human society' aid your survival?"*

B. *"How could you aid the survival of 'human society'?"*

A. *"How could 'lifeforms on earth' aid your survival?"*

B. *"How could you aid the survival of 'lifeforms on earth'?"*

A. *"How could 'this physical universe' aid your survival?"*

B. *"How could you aid the survival of 'this physical universe'?"*

A. *"How could 'spirits' (or 'entities') aid your survival?"*

B. *"How could you aid the survival of 'spirits' (or 'entities')?"*

A. *"How could an 'infinity of creation' aid your survival?"*

B. *"How could you aid the survival of an 'infinity of creation'?"*

INFINITY & BEYOND

The *Spheres of Existence* are *systematically designed* and they relate to the other *seven-plus-one* models we use to gain a better understanding of our *Systemology.* In many ways, the *Spheres* are directly or observably demonstrable as progressively *larger* or *widening* "spheres" that encompass the *Body/individual* by necessity.

If you eliminate any *one* from the *"equation"* then the *lower* ones are also removed from *existence.* Therefore, having a *Body* (maintaining its optimum *survival* in *Beta-Existence*) is dependent on the *existence* of the *higher spheres* (hence *"Spheres of Existence"*). If you eliminate *"humans"* as a *species,* you eliminate *"human groups"* and obviously any individual *"humans."* Too greatly disrupting the ability to sustain an ecosystem for *"all lifeforms on earth"* will also dampen *"human"* existence; as is progressively being felt today on *Earth.*

Our purpose in emphasizing the *"Spheres"* is to enable a *Seeker* to *play* the *"Game"* here better. Of course, beyond this, as an *Actualized Alpha-Spirit,* our hope is that they would eventually *"ascend"*—rise above the entrapment within *this Existence* and be able to *create* a better *game* elsewhere—in an even higher *Universe.*

When we approach *"Infinity"* from the perspective of the *Human Condition* in

Beta-Existence, we find the *Spheres of Existence*. Regardless of how someone might label or classify them, they are *systematically exactly* as described in our model. But as a *Seeker* reaches further on the *Pathway*, they find that the *Alpha* states and *Infinity* actually encompass more than what is immediately perceived at the start of the *journey*.

A *Seeker* will be the first to *realize* that "*To Survive*" is not the *only* possible *game* that an *Alpha-Spirit* is capable of. In fact, taking the whole *Backtrack* into *consideration*, it is probably the lowest-rung of potential *game-goals* we've experienced in our long existence. When we discover the original native purpose or goal of an *Alpha-Spirit*, we realize that our preferred activity is "*To Create*."

Infinity is the "destination point" on the "horizon" that we use to align the direction of the *Pathway*. Of course, *Infinity* is always *Infinity*. But, from a *Human*, "mortal" or "Beta" perspective, *Alpha* states and *Infinity* are practically everything that is outside, or *exterior to, Beta-Existence*. The same model-style of *"spheres within spheres"* is often also used to represent *"Universes within Universes."*

When we break free of our *reality-agreements* for *this Physical Universe*, we do not suddenly arrive at *"Infinity"* in a literal or absolute sense; we arrive at a *higher-level Universe* with a *higher-level game-goal*, from which our *"Pathway-to-Infinity"* still continues. This reaffirms that *everything* that is beyond *Beta-Existence* is essentially *Alpha* by relative comparison.

When the *Alpha-Spirit* operates a *viewpoint* from within the next highest *"Universe,"* then *that Universe* is perceived as *"Beta"* relative to whatever *exceeds*, or *is exterior to*, it. A *Seeker* would then have to take what they achieved already from the *Pathway* in *the Physical Universe* to go further with it *there*—likely having to apply a similar regimen of *defragmentation* from the *viewpoint* of an *Alpha-Spirit* while *in* the *Magic Universe*.

THE ARCS OF INFINITY

Some *Alpha* qualities may be *systematically* worked out—using our models and lore—while still in *Beta-Existence*. This is because we know that the basic structure repeats itself at a higher-level—meaning, from our perspective, a *higher "harmonic"* or *"octave."* The *"dynamics"* represented by eight *Spheres of Existence* repeat from an *Alpha* perspective, with qualities that are not inherently within *the Physical Universe*. They cannot be appropriately called *"spheres."* Since they extend beyond (or encompass) what we consider *Infinity* from a *Beta* perspective, we refer to them as the eight *"Arcs of Infinity"* for our *Systemology*.

9. (Arc 1): Ethics

10. (Arc 2): Aesthetics/Beauty

11. (Arc 3): Construction/Building

12. (Arc 4): Reason/Logic

13. (Arc 5): Variety/Randomness

14. (Arc 6): Games/Universes

15. (Arc 7): Understanding

16. (Arc 8): Creation

We *consider* the *"Arcs of Infinity"* as a *higher* "harmonic" or "octave" of the *Spheres of Existence* because, for example: "ETHICS" regards the "optimum actions" that enhance the likelihood of *survival as a* "PHYSICAL BODY." The idea and reasoning behind *"ethical action"* is not inherently a part of *this Physical Universe.* Those particular "thoughts"—or *intentions for action*—are not found within the motor-functions or "brain" of a *Body,* which when left to itself operates solely on *stimulus-response.* Those *higher considerations* are *"Alpha"* qualities because they *originate* from outside of, *or exterior to,* this *Beta-Existence.*

When we think of the *Second Sphere* of "HOME" as including loving and close intimate relationships (which are more "emotional" in nature), it is not difficult to see its connection to *game-goals* of the former *Magic Universe* ("*To Enjoy*"), which emphasized sensual pleasure. The *Second Arc* is "AESTHETICS" (which is also to say "beauty")—and here again we see a domain of "*thought*" or *consideration* that originates beyond what is contained exclusively within *the Physical Universe.*

By themselves, the *Spheres of Existence* and *Arcs of Infinity* are simply the basic structure of a *game* that we may have once even participated in *creating.* This alone is not the source of our *fragmentation.* But these *games* did, and do, provide the *foundations* or *platforms* by which additional *implanting* and *programming* is laid in—and upon which even more *imp-*

rinting and *fragmented considerations* compound on top of (or attach to). This means that many "positive" *goals* and *expressions* have only become *fragmented* by being used negatively.

Use the labels given for each of the *Arcs of Infinity* and insert them (one at a time) into the PCL-*formula* that follows:

A. *"How could your ---- enhance the survival of others?"*

B. *"How could someone else's ---- enhance your survival?"*

By *defragmenting* our *considerations* and regaining *spiritual abilities* of these *"higher"* aspects (or *Arcs*) in *this lifetime*, we not only stabilize and increase our own progress on the *Pathway*, but also *enhance* the *conditions* of *survival* while still in *this Game*. By enhancing them and ceasing to use them against one another *first*, we "unlock" or "unfold" more of our potential *thereafter*. But the *"livingness"* that we

47

experience becomes more optimal all along. We do not have to *"suffer"* in *this Life* in order to have some better tomorrow *"somewhere else."* [That particular idea is just one example of *"implanting"* on a *"religious"* level.]

Use the labels again for this PCL-*formula*:

A. *"How might making a choice based on increasing ---- lead to an optimum action?"*

B. *"How might making a choice based on increasing ---- lead to an undesirable (or harmful) action?"*

By *"optimum action"* we are indirectly referencing *Ethics*, which is the *First Arc*. The subjects of *Ethics* and *Aesthetics* are probably easiest to handle in a single lesson for *Systemology Level-6*. Many of the other areas are introduced throughout the *Professional Course*. *Ethics* and *Aesthetics* also most closely relate to *this Physical Universe* and the *Magic Universe*, which are the two main *"Universes"* we've covered on this course.

"COURAGE" & "BEAUTY"

Let's begin by *inspecting* some of the qualities inherent in the *lower "Arcs."* For example: our conception of *"courage"* became *fragmented* early on the *Backtrack* by glorifying how *beautiful* it was to be *courageous*, which—for the *Games-Universes*—meant to *"fight against overwhelming odds and lose."* [Because as we've seen in former lessons, these *Universal-Games* are designed so that everyone loses.]

At these *advanced processing-levels*, we take some of the "charge" off of the *effects* from these early obscure *implants* by *"Imagining"* a *facsimile-copy* (or an *approximation*) of whatever we are treating—or by *"Getting a Sense"* of some concept *real* enough to actually *process* it. Some of this is a far-reach in ability for *Seekers* early on, which is why we prefer to handle *"Conceptual Processing"* after effectively completing lower *processing-levels.*

In this case, let us introduce one example for *processing-out* the *"postulate"* (or *"Alpha-Thought"*) that: *"one's opponents are stronger when one is being courageous."* Run the following PCL in series repeatedly until you feel no *inclination* or *tendency* to want to *"make an opponent stronger to show off how courageous you are."*

A. *"Get a sense of the beauty of being courageous and losing."*

B. *"Get a sense of the beauty of someone else being courageous and losing."*

C. *"Get a sense of the beauty of being courageous and winning."*

D. *"Get a sense of the beauty of someone else being courageous and winning."*

Now: *Imagine* the *"feeling"* of *being strong* and *courageous* without the need to face any opponents in order to prove anything. [If this seems difficult, there may be more *"charge"* on the area, which means *running* the previous PCL-series longer.] The purpose is to regain and retain the actual characteristic of *"courage"* —which is technically, *"the ability to confront or willingly face anything"* — without the *fragmentation* attached.

Once this is accomplished: using your experience with techniques from earlier lessons; *Imagine clouds* of this *clear/pure/true courage* all around you, and absorb them into the *Body*. Additionally, practice doing this around others, or groups of people, as a *cloud* above and/or surrounding them. In *Zu-Vision*: *Imagine* these *clouds* above large cities, countrysides, nations and even the entire planet.

Although these exercises employ *creations* that only *you* are *agreeing to* as a *reality*: if the true and pure *intention* (of *"courage"*) has been *realized* (or *"contact-*

ed") and is being used here, then it *is* an effective *process* for, at the very least, your own benefit (or progress). This is one way of handling the *Arcs* for this course.

Often the idea (or *concept*) of "*beauty*" is also attached to "pristine states" or "newness." One would note this to be in effect, at a physical level, regarding our *perception* of the "*young.*" One way this is handled in *processing* is to *run* the idea (or *concept*) of "*decay*" and gradually increase a *Seeker's* "acceptance levels" of it.

For example: *Look* around the *room*; *Spot* an *object*; and *Imagine* a *facsimile-copy* of it. Throw a few away and keep at it until you are satisfied with one (rather than trying to make an existing one more vivid). Then: *Imagine* (*visualize*) your *copy* as decaying (rusting, collapsing, deteriorating, &tc.) until it breaks apart completely into a bunch of shattered *fragments*. Then: *run* this in reverse; having the *fragments* come back together (and "heal") until it matches the original state again. Alternate this several times on one *object*; then select a different *object*. This is *run* until a *Seeker* can *confront "decay."*

To advance this further: a *Seeker* applies the above steps conceptually to *living beings* (trees, animals, other people); starting with those that can be *viewed* physically, and then using *imagination* (or *ZU-Vision*) to conceive of *living beings decayed* that are not physically present. This can be applied to *larger systems*, too—*confronting* the *"decay"* of cities, civilizations, planets, galaxies and even *Universes*.

An *end-goal* of *Systemology Level-6* is for a *Seeker* to be able to *perceive, think,* and *evaluate "freely"* on a moment-to-moment basis, in their *present-time* experience of *Existence*. *Beta-Defragmentation* does not automatically "release" one from *this Game-Universe*; but a *Seeker* experiences a sense of "release" while *in this Game*, when they can fully recognize that they

do not actually need to *fight for survival*—
at which point much of the other *turbulence*, and struggles with remaining *fragmented* areas, just starts to "*fall away*."

THE ARC OF "AESTHETICS"

Aesthetics is an *Alpha*-quality *consideration*
about *how* something *is* or *appears to be*. It
is not enough to simply call it "*beauty*,"
although that is one of its areas or aspects. Our conception of what is "*beautiful*" compared to what is "*repulsive*" is a
reactive quality contained in most *fragmentation* in *this Universe* (and also, at the
very least, the *Magic Universe*).

We tend to consider "*aesthetics*" and "*art*"
to be "*positive*" *expressions* of *creative ability*; and they *are*—when they are not *fragmented*, or blatantly used *against others*.
Beauty/Ugliness can quite easily enhance
the *fragmentation* connected to *reactive*

"*reach*" and "*withdrawal.*" We can be easily *compelled* to interact, *communicate, agree, &tc.* with those that we find "*attractive*" (for whatever underlying reasons we might make that determination), even if it is not in our "best" interests. *Politics* (*marketing* and *social opinion*) can be won this way; fidelity of strong relationships can disintegrate under its effects; the list goes on.

As cliché as it has become among the speech of independent artists: the first taste of this *Arc* is often glimpsed when one is truly "taken aback" or "fascinated by" the sudden impact of true "*beauty in the world.*" This is something that is not innate to primitive survival and is not subject to reasoning or critical thought. This is one reason *aesthetics* remains an "*Alpha*" quality; because there is no equivalent "program" for it built into the systems of *the Physical Universe*. *Aesthetics* is the very thing that differentiates what is *"beautiful"* from an *"ordinary mundane creation."* And *that determination* can only come from an *Alpha-Spirit.*

For a *Seeker* to *analyze* any such *considerations,* use the following PCL; list readily available responses ("B") and then repeat "A" with something different. All we are doing here is bringing some things *up* to examine.

A. *"Recall something aesthetic (or beautiful)."*

B. *"Spot something about it that contributes to the aesthetic/beauty."*

While elements specific to *this Physical Universe* might seem inconsequential at *higher-levels*—such as to a *spiritual entity outside of it* at the *Seventh Sphere of Existence*—the *Arcs of Infinity* are introduced at the end of the *Professional Course* as suggestions for further *Alpha-Defragmentation* (which is the next main focus on the *Pathway* once a *Seeker* has successfully completed the work described in the *Professional Course* lessons).

Aesthetics have even more impact (or "power") at a *Spiritual/Alpha* level. In an *existence* where the higher *goal* is *"To Create,"* aesthetics are a major component of getting others to accept one's *creations*, or when trying to *create effects* on others. So, there is a lot of jealousy, manipulation, and critical evaluation attached to our experience of *aesthetics*. Here, a *Seeker* can *run* the following PCL to *confront* some of the *"charge"* in this area.

AESTHETICS (ENFORCED)

1. *"Recall (en)forcing an aesthetic on another."*

2. *"Recall someone (en)forcing an aesthetic on you."*

3. *"Recall someone (en)forcing an aesthetic on another."*

0. *"Recall (en)forcing an aesthetic on yourself."*

AESTHETICS (INHIBITED)

1. *"Recall inhibiting an aesthetic for another."*
2. *"Recall someone inhibiting an aesthetic for you."*
3. *"Recall someone inhibiting an aesthetic for another."*
0. *"Recall inhibiting an aesthetic for yourself."*

And then balance the above by *running* "positive action" (below) to end this cycle of *processing*.

1. *"Recall someone enjoying an aesthetic that you shared with them."*
2. *"Recall enjoying an aesthetic that someone shared with you."*
3. *"Recall someone enjoying an aesthetic that another shared with them."*
0. *"Recall enjoying an aesthetic you discovered for yourself."*

As before with *"enforcement/inhibition,"*

we will *run* "*evaluation/invalidation*" on this area; but instead of treating an *aesthetic-item* itself, this *process* pertains to *considerations* (*opinions, &tc.*) of what *is* aesthetic (or *beautiful*). "*Evaluating*" is giving the "*opinion*"; and "*Invalidating*" is negating an "*opinion.*"

AESTHETICS (EVALUATED)

1. "*Recall (en)forcing an evaluation of an aesthetic on another.*"

2. "*Recall someone (en)forcing an evaluation of an aesthetic on you.*"

3. "*Recall someone (en)forcing an evaluation of an aesthetic on another.*"

0. "*Recall (en)forcing an evaluation of an aesthetic on yourself.*"

AESTHETICS (INVALIDATED)

1. "*Recall invalidating an aesthetic for another.*"

2. "*Recall someone invalidating an aesthetic for you.*"

3. *"Recall someone invalidating an aesthetic for another."*

0. *"Recall invalidating an aesthetic for yourself."*

Then, as before, we balance this type of emphasis by *running* some positive action, such as *encouragement*.

1. *"Recall encouraging someone's creation of aesthetics."*

2. *"Recall someone encouraging your creation of aesthetics."*

3. *"Recall someone encouraging another's creation of aesthetics."*

0. *"Recall encouraging yourself to create aesthetics."*

In practical application: the first step to any area of *creation* is simply *"To Create."* This means *being creative* without the concern of *aesthetics*, *quality* or *content*. Just as one's ability to *knowingly create "mental images"* improves with practice, so do other areas. For example: if you want to "write," then just start writing a lot, for yourself, until you find it easy to sit and write. Afterward, you can begin to work on *creating writing* that *others* would want to read. In other words: start with the *creative ability*, then add the *aesthetics*. This can really be applied to any "artistic" or "creative" endeavor.

BASIC ALPHA-DEFRAGMENTATION

A *Seeker's* starting point for *"Alpha-Defragmentation"* is to be found with the *Arcs of Infinity*. Obviously, this lesson is only the beginning to a full handling of these areas. These areas extend much further on the *Backtrack* than what we even have to deal with concerning the *"Physical Body"* and this *"Beta-Existence."* This also means that as a *Seeker* advances solidly on the *Pathway*, more will become *accessible* for *inspection* because an individual is *willing* to *confront* more and more of what has been overlooked or forgotten.

Since we have already examined *Ethics* and *Aesthetics* to some extent, let's take a look at the other *Arcs*.

In traditional *defragmentation processing*, we avoid the word "*think*" in our PCL to avoid triggering or activating unnecessary *mental machinery* and *circuitry*. *Systematic Processing* is focused and targeted; it doesn't involve a lot of "freewheeling thought" if the *processes* are to be effective. However, the *processes* below are basic explorations into these *Arcs*—simply permitting a *Seeker* to get a view of each area.

A. "*Think of something you would have fun building.*"

B. "*Think of something someone else would have fun building.*"

A. "*Think of an interesting logic-puzzle you would have fun solving.*"

B. *"Think of an interesting logic-puzzle someone else would have fun solving."*

A. *"Think of some interesting changes that would be fun to have."*

B. *"Think of some interesting changes that would be fun for another."*

A. *"Think of some games that you would have fun playing."*

B. *"Think of some games that someone else would have fun playing."*

A. *"Think of something that you would find interesting to understand."*

B. *"Think of something that someone else would find interesting to understand.*

A. *"Think of something that would be interesting to create."*

B. *"Think of something that someone else would find interesting to create."*

While it is easy to see the "positive characteristics" inherent within these *Arcs*, there is unfortunately the *other side* of them for us also to *confront*. We have *all* used these *Arcs* against each other, at one time or another, on the *Backtrack*. The *lower-level control* mechanisms—like *"pain"*—really have no effect on a *godlike being*. But the *Arcs*, on the other hand— *ethics, aesthetics, building, games, &tc.—are* of extreme interest to *godlike beings*.

All of the *Arcs*—not just *"aesthetics/beauty"*—can be, and have been, used as *"lures"* for entrapment. And early on the *Backtrack*, the *Alpha-Spirit* is quite "innocent" and can be easily *"tricked."* These *Arcs* serve as the desirable *"bait"* used for laying in *higher-level fragmentation*—*"Spirit-Traps"* and *"Implants."* Therefore, by properly understanding them, additional data for many of the *"Implant-Platforms"* (used in *advanced processing*) are derived.

It is important to keep in perspective that we have all been participants in these areas; we have experienced both sides— and so these areas are not to be treated as "one-sided" ordeals. A *Seeker* should be prepared for *confronting* anything that "comes up" in *processing*; and even at *Systemology Level-6*, only some of the *most accessible* content (or "*almost knowns*") will be available for *processing* on the first pass through the course.

PCL for these *advanced processes* (below) employ the phrase "*Spot the impulse.*" This is meant to result in the *recall* of a particular "*consideration*" or "*intention,*" but can also regard a specific "*incident.*" In the absence of anything accessible: a *Seeker* may choose to "soften up" an area first by using "*Get a sense of*" as a *resurfacing* technique. The basic "*Hot Button*" (or "*keyword*") we will use for these *processes* is "*control (or manipulate).*" These *processes* use high-level *Awareness* to *defragment* by *inspecting* some tendency "*As-It-Is.*"

A. "*Spot the impulse to control (or manipulate) others through their sense of ethics.*"

B. *"Spot the impulse of others to control (or manipulate) you through your sense of ethics."*

A. *"Spot the impulse to control (or manipulate) others through their desire for beauty (or aesthetics)."*

B. *"Spot the impulse of others to control (or manipulate) you through your desire for beauty (or aesthetics)."*

In this next *Arc*, "construction" could be building material structures and things, or it could be building an organization and group. A *"Free Being"* will often *join a group* to accomplish a large constructive activity.

A. *"Spot the impulse to control (or manipulate) others through their joy of constructive efforts."*

B. *"Spot the impulse of others to control (or manipulate) you through your joy of constructive efforts."*

"Logic" is an entire subject unto itself. It is

also used to entrap by manipulating an *agreement* (to which a *Seeker* should also study *"logical fallacies"*). A *"logical argument"* is meant to persuade an individual that such-and-such (a *conclusion*) is the case only because certain other things (*premises*) are agreed with as true.

A. *"Spot the impulse to control (or manipulate) others through their agreements with logical arguments."*

B. *"Spot the impulse of others to control (or manipulate) you through your agreements with logical arguments."*

An *Alpha-Spirit* exists for a very long time and is fond of *variety* and *change*, which is to sometimes say *novelty*. If an individual can be convinced that *"something else"* is just as good (or better) than what they *"have now,"* they will usually *change it* or *trade it* just for the *"fun"* or *"novelty"* of it. But sometimes an individual becomes highly resistant to all *change* on a *reactive-automated* basis simply because this "trick" has been played on them too many times.

A. *"Spot the impulse to control (or manipulate) others through their desire for change (and variety)."*

B. *"Spot the impulse of others to control (or manipulate) you through your desire for change (and variety)."*

A. *"Spot the impulse to control (or manipulate) others through their desire to have an interesting game."*

B. *"Spot the impulse of others to control (or manipulate) you through your desire to have an interesting game."*

An *Alpha-Spirit's* desire to *"understand"* can even be turned against them. Just one of the more recognizable manifestations of this is *"playing victim."* In this case, someone is trying to *convince* you that you can't really *understand* how they *feel* unless you *feel* just as *"bad"* as they are pretending to *feel.*

A. "*Spot the impulse to control (or manipulate) others through their desire to understand.*"

B. "*Spot the impulse of others to control (or manipulate) you through your desire to understand.*"

At the peak of all this is the *Arc of Creation*—which essentially also encompasses *all* of the others; just as *Infinity* encompasses *all* of the *Spheres of Existence*. The *Alpha-Spirit* loves *creations* and *creating* above all else. We *imagine* "things" and make *facsimile-copies* of "things" just to *have things*.

To some extent, the *Pathway* is graded by an increase of *creative ability*—and by this, we mean the *certainty* a *Seeker* has on *having things*. Otherwise, they will not "let go" of some *fragmentation*. At the root of it all, an *Alpha-Spirit* is afraid of not *having enough variety* and *richness* to their *creations*. As a result, we can be tricked into *copying* and *creating* "undesirable" *reality-*

agreements just to keep a "library" of "interesting details."

A. "*Spot the impulse to control (or manipulate) others through their desire to create (or experience an interesting reality).*"

B. "*Spot the impulse of others to control (or manipulate) you through your desire to create (or experience an interesting reality).*"

Proper *defragmentation* of any area treated on the *Pathway* does not result in an *abandonment* or *withdrawal*. It results in rehabilitating the *true abilities* or *clear characteristics* by shedding the debris that enshrouds them. This is why we balance handling *deeper* or more *turbulent* areas with "*Spotting*" positive action. Rather than apply "*objective processing*" for these areas, a *Seeker* should look over the "*Arcs*" (list) and *knowingly* practice ways to *actually* develop in these areas during this lifetime, however trivial a particular activity may seem.

CREATING "INFINITIES"

At the end of the previous lesson, we presented an *advanced visualization* exercise for conceiving of "an infinite roadway." Here, we pick up from where we left off (and a *Seeker* may wish to review that material before continuing).

• *Imagine* (*create/visualize*) a "*grain of sand*." *Look* at it closely; *Notice* some of its details (exact shape, texture, color).

–Now: *Imagine* a *dozen* different individual "*grains of sand*"; making each a slightly different shape, texture, or color.

–Now: *Imagine* *thousands* of *copies* of these different individual "*grains of sand*," all mixed together forming a "*small area*." You should be able to perceive a "*speckled-like variety*" in the scenery rather

71

than simply an entire area of one fixed color, texture, or pattern.

• Building on what you practiced in the previous lesson: "*copy*" the "*small area*" (from the previous step) as many times as is necessary to get a sense of the "*sand*" stretching out like a large "*beach.*"

–Now (similar to how you had handled the "*road*"): *Imagine* (*create/intend*) that the "*beach*" extends out to "*infinity*" in both directions.

–Now (similar to how you had handled the "*road*"): *Move* to various "*locations*" on the "*beach*" to *get a sense* (or *certainty*) that it does continue as far as you are interested in checking it.

• *Look* around the *room*; *Spot* an *object*. *Imagine* (*create*) a *copy* of it, overlapping, but shifted just slightly to the side.

–*Imagine* (*create*) another *copy*, overlapping, but shifted slightly to the side of the last *copy*. Then: *make* many more *copies*, each one a little bit over, until they appear fanned out in a line, like "*cards.*"

–Now: *Make* as many *copies* of the "*object*" (or even the "*fanned out image*") as is necessary to *Imagine* a "*line*" of this *object* going on forever. When you've accomplished this to your satisfaction, "throw away" that *mental imagery*.

–Now, similar to the beginning step of this exercise: *Imagine* (*create*) a single *copy*; but this time, *Make* the "*infinite line*" of the *object* occur with one single "*intention*" (or "*postulate*"). If you have difficulties with this: *Imagine* the "coloration" gradually varying as the *copies* extend into the distance.

–Then *choose* a different *object* and repeat the *process*. Practice until you are comfortable "*creating infinities.*"

Finally, the following *process* assists increasing *spiritual perception*. It is appropriate for *ending-sessions* with, and also as a stand-alone exercise.

• *Look* around the *room*; *Spot* precise *"points"* (or *"spots"*) in the *"space"* of the *room*. [By this we mean in *"mid-air"* and not connected to, or touching, an *"object."*] Really *get a sense* that they are there, even though they have no *"mass"* to them.

–When you are comfortable with the previous step: *Spot* specific *"points"* (or *"spots"*) that are *outside of* the *room*. [This can be done with eyes open or closed, but it is done mentally (or with *ZU-Vision*) rather than with the *Body's Eyes*.]

–Alternately: *"Spot three points in the room"* and *"Spot three points outside the room."*

–When you *"feel good"* about the exercise: *"Get a sense of the floor/ground beneath you"* and *end-session*.

The Systemology Professional Course
continues in the final lesson booklet:
ALPHA THOUGHT

GLOSSARY

actualization : to make actual, not just potential; to bring into full solid Reality; to realize fully in *Awareness* as a "thing."

agreement (reality) : unanimity of opinion of what is "thought" to be known; an accepted arrangement of how things are; things we consider as "real" or as an "is" of "reality"; a consensus of what is real as made by standard-issue (common) participants; what an individual contributes to or accepts as "real"; in *Systemology*, a synonym for "*reality.*"

alpha : the first, primary, basic, superior or beginning of some form; in *Systemology*, referring to the state of existence operating on spiritual archetypes and postulates, will and intention "exterior" to the low-level condensation and solidarity of energy and matter as the 'physical universe' (*beta*).

alpha-spirit : a "spiritual" *Life*-form; the "true" *Self* or I-AM; the *individual*; the spiritual (*alpha*) *Self* that is animating the (*beta*) physical body or "*genetic vehicle*" using a continuous *Lifeline* of spiritual ("*ZU*") energy; an individual spiritual (*alpha*) entity possessing no physical mass or measurable waveform (motion) in the Physical Universe as itself, so it animates the (*beta*) physical body or "*genetic vehicle*" as a catalyst to experience *Self*-determined causality in effect within the *Physical Universe*; a singular unit or point of *Spiritual Awareness* that is *Aware* that it is *Aware*.

alpha thought : the highest spiritual *Self-determination* over creation and existence exercised by an Alpha-Spirit; the Alpha range of pure *Creative Ability* based on direct postulates and considerations of *Beingness*; spiritual qualities comparable to "thought" but originating in Alpha-existence, independently superior to a Mind-System.

ascension : actualized *Awareness* elevated to the point of true "spiritual existence" exterior to *beta existence*. An "Ascended Master" is one who has returned to an incarnation on Earth as an inherently *Enlightened One*, demonstrable in their words and actions; they have the ability to *Self-direct* the "Mind" and "Body" as *Self* (as a "Spirit"); and to maintain consciousness as a personal identity continuum with the same *Self-directed* control and communication of Will-Intention that is exercised, actualized and developed deliberately during one's present incarnation.

associative knowledge : significance or meaning of a facet or aspect assigned to (or considered to have) a direct relationship with another facet; to connect or relate ideas or facets of existence with one another; in traditional systems logic, an equivalency of significance or meaning between facets or sets that are grouped together, such as in $(a + b) + c = a + (b + c)$; in Systemology, erroneous associative knowledge is assignment of the same value to all facets or parts considered as related (even when they are not actually so), such as in $a = a, b = a, c = a$ and so forth without distinction.

attention : active use of *Awareness* toward a specific aspect or thing; the act of "attending" with the presence of *Self*; a direction of focus or concentration of *Awareness* along a particular channel or conduit or toward a particular terminal node or communication termination point; the Self-directed concentration of personal energy as a combination of observation, thought-waves and consideration; focused application of *Self-Directed Awareness*.

awareness : the highest sense of-and-as *Self* in knowing and being as I-AM (the *Alpha-Spirit*); the extent of beingness directed as a viewpoint (POV) experienced by *Self* as *Knowingness*.

beta (awareness) : all consciousness activity ("*Awareness*") in the "Physical Universe" (KI, in *Zuism*) or else in *beta-existence*; *Awareness* within the range of the *genetic-body*, including material thoughts, emotional responses and physical motors; personal *Awareness* of physical energy and physical matter moving through physical space and experienced as "time"; the *Awareness* held by *Self* that is restricted to an organic *Lifeform* or "*genetic vehicle*" in which it experiences causality in *beta-existence*.

beta (existence) : all manifestation in the "Physical Universe" (KI, in *Zuism*); the conditions of *Awareness* for the *Alpha-spirit* (*Self*) as a physical organic *Lifeform* or "*genetic vehicle*" in which it experiences causality in the *Physical Universe*.

charge : to fill or furnish with a quality; to supply with energy; to lay a command upon; in *Systemology*—to imbue with intention; to overspread with emotion; personal energy stores and significances entwined as fragmentation in mental images, reactive-response encoding and intellectual (and/or) programmed beliefs.

channel : a specific stream, course, current, direction or route; to form or cut a groove or ridge or otherwise guide along a specific course; a direct path; an artificial aqueduct created to connect two water bodies or water or make travel possible.

circuit : a circular path or loop; a closed-path within a system that allows a flow; a pattern or action or wave movement that follows a specific route or potential path only; in *Systemology*, "*communication processing*" pertaining to a specific *flow* of energy or information along a channel; "*feedback loop*."

communication : successful transmission of information, data, energy (&tc.) along a message line, with a reception of feedback; an energetic flow of intention to cause an effect (or duplication) at a distance; the personal energy moved or acted upon by will or else 'selective directed attention'; the 'messenger action' used to transmit and receive energy across a medium; also relay of energy, a message or signal—or even locating a personal POV (viewpoint) for the Self—along the *ZU-line*.

condense (condensation) : the transition of vapor to liquid; denoting a change in state to a more substantial or solid condition; leading to a more compact or solid form.

confront : to come around in front of; to be in the presence of; to stand in front of, or in the face of; to meet "face-to-face" or "face-up-to"; additionally, in *Systemology*, to fully tolerate or acceptably withstand an encounter with a particular manifestation without an automatic reactive response.

consideration : careful analytical reflection of all aspects; deliberation; determining the significance of a "thing" in relation to similarity or dissimilarity to other "things"; evaluation of facts and importance of certain facts; thorough examination of all aspects related to, or important for, making a decision; the analysis of consequences and estimation of significance when making decisions; also in *Systemology*, the *postulate* or *Alpha-Thought* that defines the state of *beingness* for what something "*is.*"

defragmentation : the *reparation* of wholeness; collecting all dispersed parts to reform an original whole; a process of removing "*fragmentation*" in data or knowledge to provide a clear understanding; applying techniques and processes that promote a *holistic* interconnected *alpha* state, favoring observational *Awareness* of continuity in all spiritual and physical systems; in *Systemology*, a "*Seeker*" achieving actualized "*Self-Honest Awareness*" is said to be in a basic state of *beta-defragmentation*, whereas *Alpha-defragmentation* is the rehabilitation of the *creative ability*, managing the *Spiritual Timeline* and the POV of *Self* as Alpha-Spirit (I-AM).

existence : the *state* or fact of *apparent manifestation*; the resulting combination of the Principles of Manifestation: consciousness, motion and substance; continued *survival*; that which independently exists.

exterior : outside of; on the outside; in *System-ology*, we mean specifically the POV of *Self* that is *'outside of'* the *Human Condition,* free of the physical and mental trappings of the Physical Universe; a metahuman range of consideration; see also *'Zu-Vision'*.

external : a force coming from outside; inform-ation received from outside sources; in *System-ology*, the objective *'Physical Universe'* exist-ence, or *beta-existence*, that the Physical Body or *genetic vehicle* is essentially *anchored* to for its considerations of locational space-time as a dimension or POV.

fragmentation : breaking into parts and scatter-ing the pieces; the *fractioning* of wholeness or the *fracture* of a holistic interconnected *alpha* state, favoring observational *Awareness* of per-ceived connectivity between parts; *discontinu-ity*; separation of a totality into parts; in *Systemology*, a person outside of *Self-Honesty* is said to be operating from a *fragmented* state.

flow : movement across (or through) a channel (or conduit); a direction of active energetic mo-tion, typically distinguished as either an *in-flow*, *out-flow* or *cross-flow*.

genetic-vehicle : a physical *Life*-form; the phys-

81

ical (*beta*) body that is animated/controlled by the (*Alpha*) *Spirit* using a continuous *Spiritual Lifeline* (ZU); a physical (*beta*) organic receptacle and catalyst for the (*Alpha*) *Self* to operate "causes" and experience "effects" within the *Physical Universe*.

harmful-act : a counter-survival mode of behavior or action (esp. that causes harm to one of more *Spheres of Existence*)—or—an overtly aggressive (hostile and/or destructive) action against an individual or any other *Sphere of Existence*; in *Utilitarian Systemology*—a shortsighted (serves fewest/lowest *Spheres of Existence*) intentional overtly harmful action to resolve a perceived problem; a revision of the rule for standard *Utilitarianism* for Systemology to distinguish actions which provide the least benefit to the least number of *Spheres of Existence*, or else the greatest harm to the greatest number of *Spheres of Existence*; in *moral philosophy*—an action which can be experienced by few and/or which one would not be willing to experience for themselves (*theft, slander, rape, &tc*); an iniquity or iniquitous act.

hold-back : withheld communications (esp. actions) such as "*Hold-Outs*"; intentional (or automatic) withdrawal (as opposed to reach); Self-restraint (which may eventually be enforced or automated); not reaching, acting or expressing, when one should be; an ability that is now restrained (on automatic) due to inability to withhold it on Self-determinism alone.

hold-outs : in photography, the numerous snapshots/pictures withheld from the final display or professional presentation of the event; withheld communications; in Utilitarian Systemology—energetic withdrawal and communication breaks with a "*terminal*" and its *Sphere of Existence* as a result of a "*Harmful-Act*"; unspoken or undiscovered (hidden, covert) actions that an individual withholds communications of, fearing punishment or endangerment of *Self-preservation* (*First Sphere*); the act of hiding (or keeping hidden) the truth of a "*Harmful-Act*"; a refusal to communicate with a *Pilot*; also "*Hold-Back.*"

holistic : the examination of interconnected systems as encompassing something greater than the *sum* of their "parts."

Human Condition : a standard default state of Human experience that is generally accepted to be the extent of its potential identity (*beingness*) —currently treated as *Homo Sapiens Sapiens,* but which is scheduled for replacement by *Homo Novus* (the "New Human").

imagination : ability to create *mental imagery* in one's Personal Universe at will and change or

83

alter it as desired; the ability to create, change and dissolve mental images on command or as an act of will; to create a mental image or have associated imagery displayed (or "conjured") in the mind that may or may not be treated as real (or memory recall) and may or may not accurately duplicate objective reality; to employ *creative abilities* of the Spirit that are independent of reality agreements with beta-existence.

imprint : to strongly impress, stamp, mark (or outline) onto a softer 'impressible' substance; to mark with pressure onto a surface; in *Systemology*, used to indicate permanent Reality impressions marked by frequencies, energies or interactions experienced during periods of emotional distress, pain, unconsciousness, loss, enforcement, or something antagonistic to physical (personal) survival, all of which are are stored with other reactive response-mechanisms at lower-levels of *Awareness* as opposed to the active memory database and proactive processing center of the Mind; an experiential "memory-set" that may later resurface—be triggered or stimulated artificially—as Reality, of which similar responses will be engaged automatically; holographic-like imagery "stamped" onto consciousness as composed of energetic *facets* tied to the "snap-shot" of an experience.

imprinting incident : the first or original event

instance communicated and *emotionally en-coded* onto an individual's "*Spiritual Timeline*" (recorded memory from all lifetimes), which formed a permanent impression that is later used to mechanistically treat future contact on that channel; the first or original occurrence of some particular *facet* or mental image related to a certain type of *encoded response*, such as pain and discomfort, losses and victimization, and even the acts that we have taken against others along the *Spiritual Timeline* of our existence that caused them to also be *Imprinted*.

intention : directed application of Will; to intend (have "in Mind") or signify (give "significance" to) for or toward a particular purpose; in *Systemology* (from the *Standard Model*)—the spiritual activity at WILL (5.0) directed by an *Alpha Spirit* (7.0); the application of WILL as "Cause" from a higher order of Alpha Thought and consideration (6.0).

interior : inside of; on the inside; in *Systemology*, we mean specifically the POV of *Self* that is fixed to the *'internal' Human Condition,* including the *Reactive Control Center* (RCC) and Mind-System or *Master Control Center* (MCC); within *beta-existence*.

internal : a force coming from inside; information received from inside sources; in *Systemology*, the objective experience of *beta-existence* associated with the Physical Body or *genetic vehicle* and its POV regarding sensation and perception; from inside the body; in the body.

invalidate : decrease the level or degree or *agreement* as Reality.

mental image : a subjectively experienced "picture" created and imagined into being by the Alpha-Spirit (or at lower levels, one of its automated mechanisms) that includes all perceptible *facets* of totally immersive scene, which may be forms originated by an individual, or a "facsimile-copy" ("snap-shot") of something seen or encountered; a duplication of wave-forms in one's Personal Universe as a "picture" that mirror an "external" Universe experience, such as an *Imprint*.

perception : internalized processing of data received by the *senses*; to become *Aware of* via the senses.

pilot : a professional steersman responsible for healthy functional operation of a ship toward a specific destination; in *Systemology*, an intensive trained individual qualified to specially apply *Systemology Processing* to assist other *Seekers* on the *Pathway*.

point-of-view (POV) : a point to view from; an opinion or attitude as expressed from a specific identity-phase; a specific standpoint or vantage-point; a definitive manner of consideration specific to an individual phase or identity; a place or position affording a specific view or vantage; circumstances and programming of an individual that is conducive to a particular response, consideration or belief-set (paradigm); a position (consideration) or place (location) that provides a specific view or perspective (subjective) on experience (of the objective).

postulate : to put forward as truth; to suggest or assume an existence *to be*; to state or affirm the existence of particular conditions; to provide a basis of reasoning and belief; a basic theory accepted as fact; in *Systemology*, Alpha-Thought —the top-most decisions or considerations made by the Alpha-Spirit regarding the "*is-ness*" (what things "are") about energy-matter and space-time.

presence : a quality of some thing (*energy/matter*) being "present" in space-time; personal orientation of *Self* as an *Awareness* (*POV*) located in present space-time (environment) and communicating with extant energy-matter.

processing command line (PCL) : a directed input; a specific command using highly selective language for *Systemology Processing*; a predetermined directive statement (cause) intended to focus concentrated attention (effect).

processing, systematic : the inner-workings or "through-put" result of systems; in *Systemology*, a method of applied spiritual technology used toward personal Self-Actualization; methods of selective directed attention, communicated language and associative imagery that increases personal control of the human condition.

realization : the clear perception of an understanding; a consideration or understanding on what is "actual"; to make "real" or give "reality" to so as to grant a property of "beingness" or "being as it is"; the state or instance of coming to an *Awareness*; in *Systemology*, "gnosis" or true knowledge achieved during *systematic processing*; achievement of a new (or higher) cognition, true knowledge or perception of Self; a consideration of reality or assignment of meaning.

responsibility : the *ability* to *respond*; the extent of mobilizing *power* and *understanding* an individual maintains as *Awareness* to enact *change*; the proactive ability to *Self-direct* and make decisions independent of an outside authority.

Seeker : an individual on the *Pathway to Self-Honesty*; a practitioner of *Mardukite Systemology* or *Systemology Processing*, that is working toward *Spiritual Ascension*.

Self-actualization : bringing the full potential of the Human spirit into Reality; expressing full capabilities and creativeness of the *Alpha-Spirit*.

Self-determinism : the freedom to act, clear of external control or influence; the personal control of Will to direct intention.

Self-honesty : the basic or original *alpha* state of *being* and *knowing*; clear and present total *Awareness* of-and-as *Self*, in its most basic and true proactive expression of itself as *Spirit* or *I-AM*—free of artificial attachments, perceptive filters and other emotionally-reactive or mentally-conditioned programming imposed on the human condition by the systematized physical world; the ability to experience existence without judgment.

spiritual timeline : a continuous stream of moment-to-moment *Mental Images* (or a record of experiences) that defines the "past" of a spiritual being (or *Alpha-Spirit*) and which includes impressions (*imprints, &tc.*) from all life-incarnations and significant spiritual events the being has encountered; in Systemology, also "*backtrack*."

Spheres of Existence : a series of *eight* concentric circles, rings or spheres (each larger than the former) that is overlaid onto the Standard Model of Beta-Existence to demonstrate the dynamic systems of existence extending out from the POV of Self (often as a "body") at the *First Sphere*; these are given in the basic eightfold systems as: *Self, Home/Family, Groups, Humanity, Life on Earth, Physical Universe, Spiritual Universe* and *Infinity-Divinity.*

Systemology : a modern tradition of applied religious philosophy and spiritual technology based on *Arcane Tablets* (in combination with "*general systemology*" and "*games theory*") developed in the New Age underground by Joshua Free in 2011 as an advanced futurist extension of the *Mardukite Research Org.*

terminal (node) : a point, end, or mass, on a line; a connection point for closing an electric circuit, such as a post on a battery terminating at each end of its own systematic function; a point of connectivity with other points; in systems, a contact point of interaction; a point of interaction with other points.

turbulence : a quality or state of distortion or disturbance that creates irregularity of a flow or pattern; the quality or state of aberration on a line (such as ragged edges) or the emotional "turbulent feelings" attached to a particular flow or terminal node; a violent, haphazard or disharmonious commotion (such as in the ebb of gusts and lulls of wind action).

validation : a reinforcement of agreements or considerations as being "real."

viewpoint : see *"point-of-view" (POV)*.

willingness : the state of conscious Self-determined ability and interest (directed attention) to *Be, Do* or *Have*; a Self-determined consideration to reach, face up to (*confront*) or manage some "mass" or energy; the extent to which an individual considers themselves able to participate, act or communicate along some line, to put attention or intention on the line, or to produce (create) an effect.

ZU : the ancient Sumerian cuneiform sign for the archaic verb—*"to know," "knowingness"* or *"awareness"*; in *Mardukite Zuism and Systemology*, the active energy/matter of the "Spiritual Universe" (AN) experienced as a *Lifeforce* or *consciousness* that imbues living forms extant in the "Physical Universe" (KI); *"Spiritual Life Energy"*; energy demonstrated by the WILL of an actualized *Alpha-Spirit* in the "Spiritual Universe" (AN), which impinges its *Awareness* into the Physical Universe (KI), animating/controlling *Life* for its experience of *beta-existence* along an individual Alpha-Spirit's personal *Identity-continuum*, called a *ZU-line*.

Zu-Line : a theoretical construct in *Mardukite Zuism and Systemology* demonstrating *Spiritual*

Life Energy (*ZU*) as a personal individual "con-tinuum" of Awareness interacting with all Spheres of Existence on the Standard Model of Systemology; a spectrum of potential variations and interactions of a monistic continuum or sin-gular *Spiritual Life Energy* demonstrated on the Standard Model; an energetic channel of poten-tial POV and "locations" of Beingness, demon-strated in early Systemology materials as an individual Alpha-Spirit's personal *Identity- con-tinuum*, potentially connecting *Awareness* of *Self* with "*Infinity*" simultaneous with all points considered in existence; a symbolic demonstra-tion of the "*Life-line*" on which *Awareness (ZU)* extends from the direction of the "Spiritual Uni-verse" (AN) in its true original *alpha state* through an entire possible range of activity res-ulting in its *beta state* and control of a *genet-ic-entity* occupying the *Physical Universe (KI).*

Zu-Vision : the true and basic (*Alpha*) Point-of-View (perspective, POV) maintained by *Self* as *Alpha-Spirit* outside boundaries or considera-tions of the *Human Condition* and *exterior* to beta-existence reality agreements with the Phys-ical Universe; a POV of Self *as* "a unit of Spir-itual Awareness" that exists independent of a "body" and entrapment in a *Human Condition*; "spirit vision" in its truest sense.

explore the
Fundamentals of Systemology

All *six*
Basic Course
lesson booklets
in one
hardcover
edition!

start your journey on the
The Pathway to Ascension

All *sixteen*
Professional Course
lesson booklets
in two
hardcover
volumes!

THE SYSTEMOL

Seekers and students of the *Basic Course* and *Professional Course* will also be interested in the *Systemology Core Research Series*. These eight volumes are a complete chronological record of the Mardukite New Thought developments from the Systemology Society, published in 2019 through 2023.

The *Systemology Core* begins with the first professional publication released when the *Mardukite Systemology Society* emerged from the underground in 2019, with: *"The Tablets of Destiny Revelation."*

OGY PATHWAY

The Tablets of Destiny Revelation:
How Long-Lost Anunnaki Wisdom
Can Change the Fate of Humanity

Crystal Clear: *Handbook for Seekers*

Metahuman Destinations (2 *volumes*)

Imaginomicon:
Approaching Gateways to Higher Universes

Way of the Wizard: *Utilitarian Systemology*

Systemology-180: *Fast-Track to Ascension*

Systemology Backtrack:
Reclaiming Spiritual Power & Past-Life Memory

PUBLISHED BY THE **JOSHUA FREE** IMPRINT REPRESENTING

The Mardukite Academy of Systemology

THE JOSHUA FREE IMPRINT
JFI PUBLICATIONS

MARDUKITE
ZUISM

mardukite.com